IS IT science?

Flat Earth and Round Earth

Rebecca Stefoff

Cavendish Square

New York

Published in 2014 by Cavendish Square Publishing, LLC
303 Park Avenue South, Suite 1247, New York, NY 10010

Copyright © 2014 by Cavendish Square Publishing, LLC

First Edition

Website: cavendishsq.com

This publication represents the opinions and views of the author based on his or her personal experience, knowledge, and research. The information in this book serves as a general guide only. The author and publisher have used their best efforts in preparing this book and disclaim liability rising directly or indirectly from the use and application of this book.

CPSIA Compliance Information: Batch #WW14CSQ

All websites were available and accurate when this book was sent to press.

Library of Congress Cataloging-in-Publication Data
Stefoff, Rebecca.
Flat earth and round earth / by Rebecca Stefoff.
  p. cm. — (Is it science?)
Includes index.
ISBN 978-1-62712-512-3 (hardcover) ISBN 978-1-62712-513-0 (paperback)
ISBN 978-1-62712-514-7 (ebook)
1. Earth (Planet) — Juvenile literature. 2. Errors, Scientific — Juvenile literature. 3. Astronomy — History — Popular works — Juvenile literature. I. Stefoff, Rebecca, 1951-. II. Title.
QB631.4 S83 2014
525—d23

Editorial Director: Dean Miller
Senior Editor: Peter Mavrikis
Copy Editor: Cynthia Roby
Art Director: Jeffrey Talbot

Designer: Amy Greenan
Photo Researcher: Julie Alissi, J8 Media
Production Manager: Jennifer Ryder-Talbot
Production Editor: Andrew Coddington

Printed in the United States of America

IS IT science?

Contents

As if sailing off the edge of the
Earth wasn't enough to worry
about, the creator of this fantasy
map added another imaginary
danger: an immense dragon.

Flat, Round— Maybe Even Hollow

History books can be wrong. Sometimes a mistake slips in. One mistake was repeated in history books, and even in children's schoolbooks, for years and years. It was about the shape of the world and the explorer Christopher Columbus, who sailed from Europe to the Americas in 1492.

Kids in school used to learn—maybe some still *do* learn—that people in Columbus's day thought the world was flat. Only Columbus guessed the truth and realized that Earth is round. The old story says that during Columbus's long voyage across the Atlantic Ocean, his men grew restless. They were afraid their captain was leading them on a doomed adventure, and they would sail right off the edge of Earth!

Columbus's men did grow restless, but *not* because they thought Earth was flat and they were about to fall off its edge. Instead, as the voyage dragged on and on, the men worried that they might get lost and not find the way back across the ocean to their homes.

But what about the edge of Earth? Sailors in Columbus's time knew perfectly well that the world is round, not flat, and that it does not have an edge. In fact, ancient Greek scientists knew about Earth's roundness 1,500 years before Columbus was born.

In different times and places, people have held all sorts of ideas about the world on which we live. Earth has been pictured as flat, round, or shaped like a bowl or a box. Some people have even thought that the world is hollow, and that people or whole civilizations can live inside it.

Today we know that the world is round—or is it? A **sphere** is a perfectly round object, like a ball or a globe. But Earth, it turns out, is *not* a perfect sphere. The discovery of the world's true shape is a story of science in action, one that spans many centuries. To follow that story, it helps to know something about the **scientific method**.

This vision of a flat Earth has land, sea, and even ships on both sides of the coin-shaped world. Water-wheels move vessels from one side to the other.

ONE

Using the Scientific Method

Science is the search for accurate knowledge about the world. To guide them on that search, scientists rely on the scientific method, which came into wide use during the seventeenth century.

The Scientific Method

The scientific method is a process, or series of steps. There are many versions, but the basic steps are:

Observation

Research

Hypothesis

Test or Experiment

Conclusion

Share and Repeat

Observation means seeing something that raises a question. For example, ancient **astronomers** noticed that the full moon sometimes "disappeared" from the sky for a few hours. It would be shining bright silver, and then a dark curve would appear on one edge, as if someone had taken a giant bite out of a sugar cookie in the night sky. Little by little, the darkness would grow until it covered the moon's surface. Then it would slowly move away until the moon shone brightly once again. These events are called lunar eclipses, or eclipses of the moon. Ancient astronomers wanted to know what caused them.

Research means gathering data, or information, that might

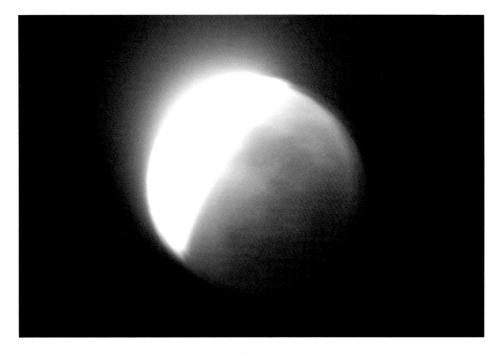

During a lunar eclipse, Earth's shadow covers part or all of the moon, turning its silvery glow to a dull reddish-brown.

answer the question. Maybe the answer is already known. If it is not known, research gives the scientist data that may lead to the answer.

To research lunar eclipses, skywatchers thousands of years ago watched these events carefully. Early astronomers were skilled skywatchers who kept detailed records of what they saw in the heavens. (Those records became the basis of calendars.) The ancient astronomers knew that the moon and sun change position in the sky over the course of a year. They saw that lunar

A solar eclipse happens when the moon passes between Earth and the sun, as in the bottom row of diagrams. The top row shows the eclipse gradually darkening the sun.

eclipses happen only when the moon and sun are in certain positions relative to each other. Once the astronomers understood how eclipses are related to the regular pattern of the sun's and moon's movements, they could predict when the next eclipse would take place.

A *hypothesis* is the next step in the scientific method. It is an educated guess based on what the scientist has observed and researched. Ancient astronomers came up with a hypothesis to explain what causes eclipses. A lunar eclipse happens when

Ancient astronomers learned to predict eclipses, caused by Earth, moon, and sun lining up in certain ways.

Peer Review

To be published in a scientific journal, an article or report must be read and approved by experts in the subject. This is called peer review. The experts who review the article do not have to agree with the conclusion of the scientist who wrote it. What matters is that the author followed the standards and procedures of the scientific method in forming the hypothesis, doing the research, and designing the experiments.

the sun, Earth, and moon line up in the sky. At such times, the moon passes through Earth's shadow. The moon has no light of its own—it shines only because it reflects the sunlight that falls on its surface. When the moon enters the shadow cast across space by Earth, the moon appears to "go out" for a while, until it moves outside the shadow zone.

Testing the hypothesis shows whether or not it is the right explanation. This part of the scientific method often involves experiments. Even when a scientist cannot actually do a particular experiment, he or she must at least be able to *think* of a way the hypothesis could be tested.

An ancient astronomer could not send a spaceship high above Earth and the moon to see whether lunar eclipses are really caused by Earth's shadow, and not by a dragon eating the moon. But the astronomer might have thought, "If a person could somehow rise high enough to look down on Earth and the moon from above, the question would be answered." This meant that the hypothesis was testable, at least in theory. A scientific hypothesis must be testable. If there is no imaginable way to test a hypothesis, it can never be proved—or disproved. That removes it from the realm of science.

One way to test a hypothesis is to ask, "If my hypothesis is correct, what other things must be true, too?" If lunar eclipses are caused by Earth's shadow blotting out the sun, for example, then the shape of Earth must match the shape of the shadow that creeps across the face of the moon. The shadow is always curved. If the hypothesis that lunar eclipses are caused by Earth's shadow is true, Earth must be round—either spherical, like a ball, or round and flat, like a plate.

A *conclusion* comes from tests and experiments. In this step, the scientist looks at the results of the experiments and asks, "Do these results support my hypothesis?"

If the answer is "no," the scientist adds the results to his or her observations, then thinks of a new hypothesis. Good scientists admit their mistakes and wrong ideas, because their goal is to be accurate and truthful. Good science is also flexible, growing and changing as new knowledge is gained.

If the answer is "yes," the scientist usually *repeats* the experiment to make sure. To be considered scientific, the result of a test or experiment has to be able to be reproduced. Scientists share their work by publishing it in **scientific journals** so that others can test it, too.

Science or Pseudoscience?

FEATURES OF SCIENCE:

- Based on scientific method
- Uses reason and logic
- Looks for physical forces to
  explain results
- Testable
- Results can be reproduced
- Published in scientific journals, and
  for the general public, too

FEATURES OF PSEUDOSCIENCE:

- Often based on tradition or folklore
- Appeals to feelings
- Explains results in mystical or mysterious ways
- May not be testable
- Results cannot be regularly reproduced
- Published for the general public, sometimes
  does not meet standards of
  scientific journals

The scientific method is a powerful way to learn about the world. It gives scientists everywhere a clear set of standards to meet. It is also an excellent tool for identifying pseudoscience.

Pseudoscience

Pseudo- (SOO-doh) at the beginning of a word means "false" or "fake." Pseudoscience is false science. It is presented as if it were scientific, but it does not meet the standards of good science.

Many pseudoscientific claims are not testable. They may be so broad or vague that they have no meaning. "Crystals have healing power" is an example of a pseudoscientific claim. A scientist examining that claim would ask, "What kind of crystals? Are diamonds better for healing than plain old rock quartz?

What illnesses is each type of crystal supposed to heal? Have crystals been tested in hospitals or laboratories?"

Pseudoscientific claims are sometimes presented as facts, but with no evidence, or with poor evidence. If there is evidence, it may be statistics or quotes with no sources. Without knowing exactly where a piece of information comes from, it's impossible to check that the source is reliable and the information is accurate.

Finally, pseudoscience is often based on beliefs and feelings rather than logic and reason. A pseudoscientific idea may spring from tradition, folklore, or even religious writings. However, the fact that an idea, claim, or belief is pseudoscience does not always mean that the idea cannot possibly be true. It only means that it is not science.

The scientific method has cast light on many mysteries and answered many questions. It is the basis for all the sciences, from **astronomy** to zoology, the study of animals. There is even one branch of science devoted completely to measuring Earth. It is called **geodesy**, or **geodetics**. Modern scientists have used geodesy to answer questions about Earth's shape and size. Long before the scientific method existed, people answered those questions in other ways: with myths and stories.

TWO

The Shapes of the World

Ancient cultures all over the world pictured the shape of Earth in pretty much the same way. Earth was a **disk**—a round, flat shape like a plate, with lumpy spots where mountains rose. This disk-shaped world floated on an ocean, or an ocean flowed around its rim like a huge river.

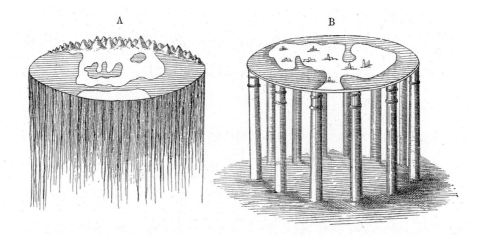

Some early ideas about the world had it resting on columns—but what did the columns rest on?

Mountains formed steep borders around many early cultures and countries. It was no wonder that people expected mountains at the rim of the world.

It's easy to see why people thought of the world this way. From wherever a person stood, the world stretched away in all directions. If the landscape was made up of plains, fields, or deserts, it was flat. In other places, hills and mountains rose toward the sky, but on the other side of them, the land was flat again. And if you traveled far enough in any direction, you came to the ocean. Nowhere did Earth's surface look like the curved surface of a ball or globe.

In time, thinkers in ancient Greece began to picture the world as a sphere. That shape explained many things they had observed, such as the fact that people in northern Greece saw different arrangements of stars in the sky than people in southern Egypt saw. Over hundreds of years, the idea of the spherical Earth took hold and spread. More and more people understood that Earth is round. By the time modern scientists were able to prove that Earth is a sphere, the idea was no longer new.

Maps, Myths, and a Hero's Shield

The world's oldest writings and maps come from ancient Egypt and from Mesopotamia, an old name for the land that is now the Middle Eastern nation of Iraq. These ancient documents show that thousands of years ago, the people of those civilizations believed that Earth was a round, flat disk. It floated like a huge island on an ocean that circled the world. The sky was a solid roof high overhead, like the inside of a bowl that has been turned upside down.

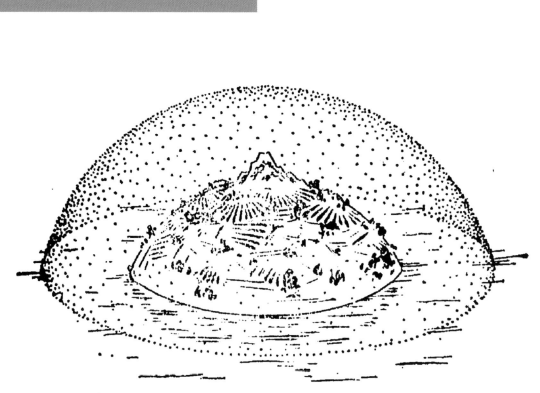

In many early beliefs, a sky dome covered the world.

The people of ancient India also believed that the world floated on an encircling ocean, but they pictured Earth a little differently. Instead of being a single flat disk, it was made up of four disks that spread out from a central mountain called Meru. A ring of mountains surrounded the far edge of the encircling ocean.

The ancient Chinese also viewed the world as flat, but they did not think it was round like a plate. They thought of it as a vast flat square, with the round dome of the heavens above it. The Norse and German peoples of northern Europe described their own view of the world in their myths and legends. To them

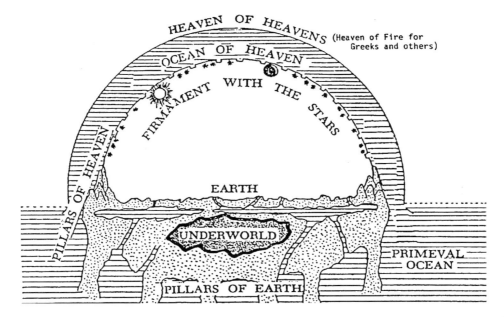

Some visions of the flat Earth had an underworld below, ocean around the edge, and fire above.

the world was flat, with a huge tree called Yggdrasil at its center. A sea flowed forever around the edge of the world, and in that sea lived an enormous snake.

Homer and Hesiod were Greek poets who probably lived and wrote around 750 BC. In their writings, they say that the world was shown on the shield of Achilles, a mighty Greek warrior and hero. Earth's continents spread across the flat shield, and the ocean flowed around its edge. To these and other Greeks of their time, the world was flat and disk-shaped. A few centuries later, Greek thinkers suggested a different shape.

Aristotle, drawn here by an artist of the
Middle Ages, had logical reasons for
thinking Earth is a sphere.

A New Idea

No one knows who the first person was to suggest that Earth is a sphere. It might have been Pythagoras, a Greek mathematician of the sixth century BC. By the fifth century BC, the spherical Earth was accepted by most major Greek thinkers and scientists. The philosopher Plato told his students that if they could soar above Earth, they would see that it is a ball. He believed that Earth was a sphere because he thought that was the perfect shape.

Plato's pupil Aristotle became a philosopher as well. He also believed that Earth is spherical, but for scientific reasons. As a person travels south, the constellations in the southern part of the sky rise higher above the horizon. This means, Aristotle saw, that Earth's surface must be curved. He wrote that Earth is a sphere with five zones of climate. The two poles are cold. A hot zone circles the middle. Between the cold and hot zones are two mild zones where people can live. The people of the northern mild zone could never meet those of the southern mild zone, however, because no one could cross the burning hot zone.

The knowledge that Earth is round became common among the Greeks and Romans. Many of their scientists and geographers mentioned the spherical Earth in their writings. One of these scholars was Claudius Ptolemy, a Greek who lived in Alexandria, Egypt, in the second century AD. His book on geography and mapmaking was a major influence for more than a thousand years. In it, Ptolemy explained that Earth is a sphere.

What Sailors See

Ptolemy and other geographers of the ancient world thought that sailors might have been the first people to realize that Earth is a sphere. That's because of the way distant objects change their appearance when seen at sea.

When a ship sails toward a mountainous coast, the first things that a sailor on the ship sees are the tops of mountains. They come into view first, followed by the lower slopes, and finally the town and harbor at the base of the mountains along the seashore. The curvature of Earth's surface means that tall things can be seen from farther away than things at sea level.

The same thing happens when a sailor catches sight of another ship on the horizon, or when someone in a harbor sees a ship approaching from the sea. If Earth were flat, the whole ship would come into view at once, from the waterline to the top of the masts or smokestacks. The only change would be that the ship would be tiny when it first appeared in the distance but would gradually appear larger as it came closer.

But that's not what happens. Instead, the first thing that appears is the top of the masts or smokestacks. The hull of the ship, where it meets the surface of the sea, is the last thing to appear. Once again, Earth's curved surface caused the highest point to be visible first.

These sights have always been part of life at sea. That's why sailors may have been the first to understand that Earth is round—and why Columbus's men would not have worried about sailing over the edge of the world.

He knew this because, as someone travels north or south, the northern or southern stars rise higher in the sky, and some stars disappear entirely. If Earth were flat, the same stars would be seen from everywhere on its surface.

Notions and Knowledge in the Middle Ages

The writings of Ptolemy and other ancient geographers traveled down through the centuries in Europe and also in the Arab world of the Middle East and North Africa. The knowledge that the world is a sphere was forgotten at times, but it was never entirely lost.

In Europe between the fourth and fourteenth centuries AD, the Christian church was the center of nearly all learning. Many

World in a Box

One Christian monk of the sixth century AD came up with an idea of the world's shape that he claimed was based on the Bible. He was called Cosmas Indicopleustes, which means "Cosmas the voyager to India." Before becoming a monk, Cosmas had been a merchant, and he had traveled from his home in Alexandria, Egypt, to India at least once. Around 550 he wrote a book saying that the world is flat and rectangular, and that it forms the bottom of a kind of box, with the curved heavens as the box's lid. Cosmas's worldview did not catch on, however, even among other Christians of his time.

Christian scholars knew and wrote that Earth is a sphere, or ball. A few disagreed. They wrote that the world was "round," but meant that it was flat and circular, like a shield or a wheel rather than a ball. In general, most educated people during the Middle Ages knew that Earth is ball-shaped. As for the mass of uneducated people, unfortunately no one bothered to record their thoughts on the shape of Earth.

Around a Round World

By the time Christopher Columbus was getting ready for his historic voyage, no one seriously thought Earth was flat. In fact, Columbus's plan depended on the fact that Earth is spherical. He wanted to reach the distant shores of Asia by sea, rather than by making the long journey over land, traveling east from Europe across all of Asia. Knowing that Earth was round, Columbus figured he could sail west from Europe and go all the way around the world to reach the eastern coast of Asia.

Columbus was right, in a way. Because Earth is a sphere, it is possible to reach the east by sailing west. But Columbus made two mistakes. First, he greatly underestimated the size of Earth. He expected to sail from Spain to China or Japan in just a few weeks, when in reality the distance is much too great for that. Second, he never considered the possibility that there might be unknown lands lying between Europe and Asia, blocking his way. So when he found land at the far side of the Atlantic Ocean from Europe, he thought he had reached Asia. Instead, he had reached the Americas, but he didn't know it.

Twenty-seven years after Columbus's first voyage, Europeans still wanted a sea route to Asia. In 1519 another explorer, Ferdinand Magellan, set out to find a way through or around those pesky American continents. He succeeded, and his fleet sailed into the Pacific Ocean and on around the world.

Magellan died during the voyage, but the survivors of his expedition finally returned to Spain in 1522. They were the first

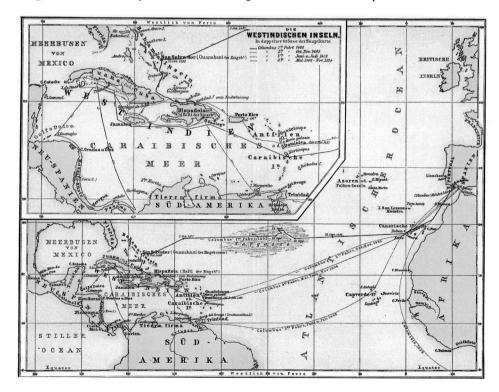

This map charts the voyages of Christopher Columbus. In four attempts, he never reached Asia— but he never sailed over the edge of the world.

people to travel completely around the world. They knew from firsthand experience that Earth is round, with no end or edge to be found.

Many people alive today have traveled around the world a different way—through space. They are the astronauts who have gone into space on missions to the moon or aboard shuttles and space stations. They have viewed the sphere of the turning Earth from high above its surface. Through videos and films made in space, they have shared that view with the world.

The route of the first voyage around the round world, commanded by Ferdinand Magellan.

THREE

Measuring and Mapping Earth

Once people had accepted the idea that Earth is a sphere, the most important question was: How big is it? The first known experiment to measure the size of Earth was carried out by a librarian in Egypt more than 2,200 years ago. Since that time, scientists have developed new tools and methods to give extremely accurate measurements of the size and shape of the world. At the same time, **cartographers**, or mapmakers, have found many ways to meet their biggest challenge: picturing a spherical world on a flat map.

The Librarian's Experiment

The librarian was named Eratosthenes. He lived in the third century BC in Alexandria, Egypt, which was a major center of learning in the ancient world. Eratosthenes is an important figure in the history of geodesy for two reasons.

First, Eratosthenes invented the system of **latitude** and **longitude**. The two measurements pinpoint the location of any spot on Earth's surface. The lines you see on a map or globe are lines of latitude and longitude. Latitude lines are horizontal. They mark a place's distance north or south of the equator, the line around the center of Earth. Longitude lines are vertical, running from pole to pole. A measurement of longitude marks a place's location east or west of the **prime meridian**, which is the line of longitude that runs through the town of Greenwich, England.

Second, Eratosthenes performed an experiment to measure the size of Earth. He had heard that at the summer solstice, the longest day of the year, the sun at noon shone straight down into a well in the city of Syene, located south of Alexandria. This meant that at that moment the sun was directly over Syene. Eratosthenes knew that Earth is round. That means that its **circumference**, or the distance around it, is also a circle. In geometry—a kind of mathematics used to measure shapes—all circles are divided into 360 degrees. Eratosthenes realized that he could use geometry to calculate the size of Earth. It worked this way: Alexandria and Syene are two points on the circle of Earth's surface. If the sun is directly over Syene at noon on the day of the summer solstice, the sun's angle there is 0 degrees. Eratosthenes measured the angle of the sun as seen from Alexandria at that very moment and found that the sun was 7.12 degrees from the center of the sky. This meant that the two cities were separated by 7.12 degrees, out of a total of 360 degrees for Earth's circumference. The distance between the two cities was known, so all Eratosthenes had to do was divide that distance by 7.12, and he would know the length of a single degree. Then he could multiply that number by 360 to get the circumference of Earth.

Eratosthenes came up with a distance of about 25,000 miles around the world. Modern scientists know that Earth's circumference is close to 24,855 miles. Using simple tools and basic math, Eratosthenes came very close to an exact measurement!

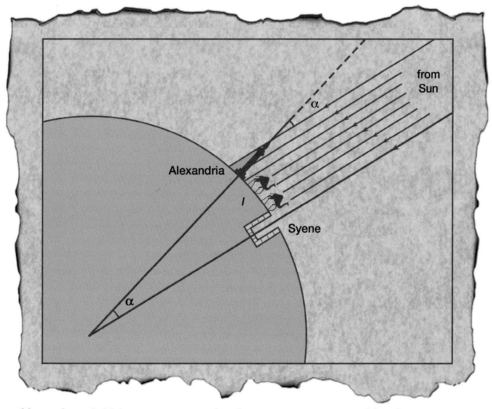

More than 2,200 years ago a simple measurement and basic geometry brought Eratosthenes close to knowing Earth's size.

Early surveyors at work. Two men in the center measure angles to a faraway tower. With the distance between the men known (see the ruler mark under their feet), they can triangulate the tower's location and height.

A couple of centuries later, the great geographer Ptolemy came up with a different number. He said that the world was about 18,000 miles around. Ptolemy's figure was repeated many times over the centuries. Explorers who relied on Ptolemy's geography thought Earth was much smaller than it really is. Columbus, for example, based his plan on Ptolemy—which meant that he expected the distance from Spain to Asia to be much, much shorter than it is.

Geodesy and the Oblate Spheroid

In the sixteenth and seventeenth centuries, scientists and surveyors started using telescopes and other instruments to make new, more accurate measurements of Earth. This was the beginning of geodesy, the study of the Earth's shape. One of the most important tools of geodesists was **triangulation**, a way of measuring Earth's surface as a series of triangles.

With triangulation, surveyors had the means to find the exact position of a distant point by measuring the angles to it from two other points that are a known distance apart.

As the great project of **surveying** Earth's surface continued, scientists realized that the planet is not a perfect sphere, meaning that it is not exactly round with every point on its surface the same distance from its center. But what *is* its true shape? Two rival theories developed.

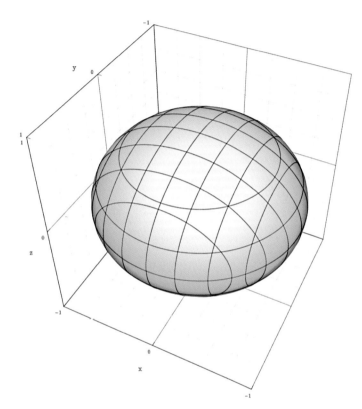

Earth's true shape is an oblate sphere, flattened a little at the poles.

French scientists thought Earth was a prolate sphere, that is, shaped like an egg. The distance between the two poles was greater than the distance through the middle of Earth. But English scientists argued that Earth was an **oblate spheroid**, meaning that it was a bit flattened at the poles, like an orange that has been slightly squished. The distance through the middle was greater than the distance between the poles.

As it turns out, the English were right. Earth is an oblate sphere, slightly flattened at the poles and bulging a little at the equator. Since the 1960s, geodesists have used space-based instruments to measure Earth's size and shape with great accuracy. Among these tools are the same Navigation Satellite Timing and Ranging Global Positioning System (NAVSTAR GPS) satellites that provide information to the GPS application's location and navigation software in cellphones and cars.

A World Inside the World?

Myths and legends from many cultures speak of an underworld, a realm beneath Earth's surface that may be entered through caves or other openings. Closer to the present day, a few people have suggested that Earth might be a hollow sphere, like an empty ball.

In the early nineteenth century, an American named John Cleves Symmes thought that Earth was not just one hollow sphere but five—one inside the other like a set of nesting dolls. Symmes claimed that Earth's surface—where the human race lives—is the outer side of a shell about 800 miles thick. Huge openings at the North Pole

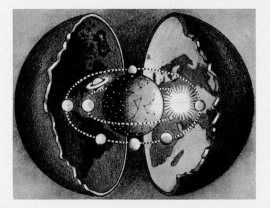

and South Pole led inward, and through these openings it would be possible for people to travel inside Earth and visit the other layers or shells within it.

Symmes and his supporters managed to get President John Quincy Adams interested in the idea of an expedition to the North Pole to not only search for the opening into Earth's center but also enter it. Sadly for the hollow-Earth believers, Adams never authorized the expedition.

By the twentieth century no scientist took seriously the idea that Earth might be hollow. However, a few mystical writers still claimed to have secret knowledge of advanced civilizations inside Earth. Some said the inner-Earth civilization was made up of survivors from the sunken continent of Atlantis. Others said that the hollow Earth housed space aliens or the descendants of wise people who had fled from the surface world ages ago.

The hollow-Earth theory also inspired writers of fiction. Edgar Allen Poe used it in his adventure story *The Narrative of A. Gordon Pym* (1838). Jules Verne's novel *Journey to the Center of the Earth* (1864) has been made into several movies. In the twentieth century, Edgar Rice Burroughs, the creator of Tarzan, wrote an entire series of books about a land he called Pellucidar, located inside the hollow Earth. The inner world is only imaginary, however. Scientists now know that below its surface, Earth is made up of layers of rock and liquid metal.

A Problem for Mapmakers

If Earth were flat after all, life would have been a lot simpler for one group of people—the cartographers. The spherical world has long been a big challenge to mapmakers.

It is impossible to represent the spherical Earth on a flat map with complete accuracy.

Imagine removing the skin of an orange in a single piece, then trying to flatten it. The skin would pucker, wrinkle, or tear. When Earth's surface is drawn on a flat surface, some aspect of it becomes distorted. Area, distance, direction, and shape cannot

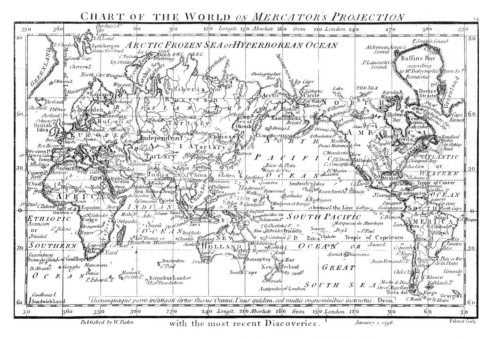

Made around 1798, this map uses the Mercator projection, which is accurate for small areas but makes land masses near the poles look bigger than they really are.

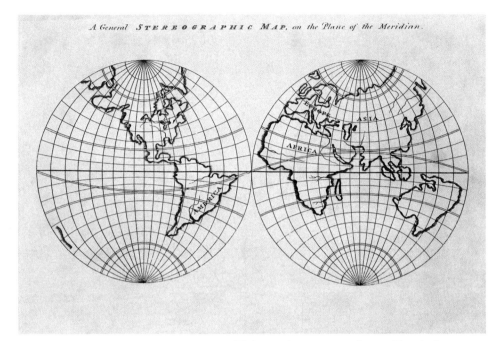

This antique map shows Earth from
two sides in a stereographic projection.

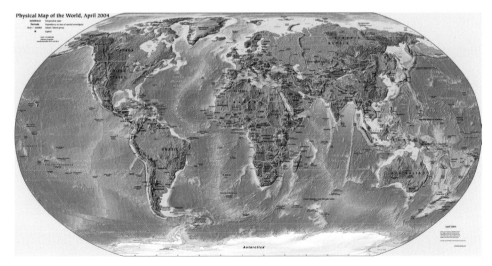

The Robinson projection is one of
the most realistic ways of drawing a
spherical world on a flat map.

**The most accurate map of our
planet is a globe. It reproduces the
shape of Earth in three dimensions.**

all be represented accurately on the same map. This is not much of a problem on maps of small areas, but it is a major problem on maps of the whole world.

To meet this challenge, mapmakers have invented a variety of **projections**, or methods of representing Earth's surface in maps. No one projection is perfect, but each works well for certain uses.

The Flat Earth Today

Strange though it may seem, a few modern people have claimed that Earth is flat, mostly for religious reasons. In the late nineteenth century, a handful of Christians in Britain and South Africa said that Earth is called flat in the Bible, and that science had not proved that untrue. An American Christian group in Zion, Illinois, made the same claim in the early twentieth century. Several Islamic sects have also described Earth as flat.

The Flat Earth Society was established in the United States in 1956 to promote belief in a flat Earth. Its founders called the spherical Earth a conspiracy by scientists and governments to fool the people. The Flat Earth Society still exists in the form of a website that claims to have more than 400 members worldwide. Some of them believe that space travel is a hoax, and that no one has ever gone to the moon or viewed Earth from space.

The Three-dimensional Map

Earth exists in three dimensions, but maps have only two dimensions. Only a three-dimensional (3D) map can represent the spherical Earth with complete accuracy. That 3D map is also a sphere. It is called a globe.

Historians know that the ancient Greeks made globes, but none of these early globes have survived. The oldest known globe in the world today was made in Germany by a navigator and geographer named Martin Behaim. The people of his hometown called the globe Behaim's *Erdapfel*, or "Earth apple."

Martin Behaim completed his work on the Earth apple in 1492—the very year that Columbus set sail westward to reach the distant east. Behaim's globe proves that even though people of Columbus's time did not know how large the world is, they knew that it is round.

When Christopher Columbus and his men sailed into the unknown, they did know one thing. They were in no danger of falling of the edge of the world.

Glossary

astronomer   a scientist who studies space and the things in it

astronomy   the scientific study of space and the things in it

cartographer   mapmaker; someone who practices cartography (the art and science of making maps)

circumference   the distance around something

disk   a round, flat shape that resembles a plate

geodesy   another name for geodetics

geodetics   the science and practice of measuring Earth, including its magnetic field

latitude   a place's distance north or south of the equator, measured in degrees; the North Pole, for example, is 90 degrees north of the equator

longitude   a place's distance east or west of a line called the prime meridian, measured in degrees; Honolulu, Hawaii, for example, is 157.8583 degrees west of the prime meridian

oblate spheroid   a sphere that is slightly flattened at the top and bottom, so that the distance through the middle is larger than the distance from top to bottom

prime meridian   the starting point for measurements of longitude; an imaginary line that runs from the North Pole to the South Pole and passes through Greenwich, England

projection   method of representing Earth's surface (which has three dimensions) on a flat map (which has two dimensions)

pseudoscience   false science; something that looks like science, or claims to be science, but isn't

scientific journals magazines that publish articles about scientific research for other scientists to read

scientific method a set of practical steps for answering questions about the world and adding to knowledge about objects and events in nature

sphere a solid, round object that has the same distance from its center to every point on its surface

surveying measuring the location of points on Earth's surface and the distances between them, for mapmaking or drawing property boundaries

triangulation a kind of surveying that divides land into a series of triangles; a surveyor who knows the exact length of one side of the triangle uses mathematics to get the lengths of the other two lines

Timeline

around 750 BC Greek poets Homer and Hesiod describe the world as flat, like the surface of a shield

400s BC Many Greek thinkers accept the idea that Earth is a sphere, or ball

around 240 BC Eratosthenes makes a nearly accurate measurement of Earth's size

100s AD	Geographer and mapmaker Ptolemy gives evidence for the spherical Earth
around 550	European traveler Cosmas Indicopleustes writes that Earth is flat, like the bottom of a box; few people share his idea
1492–1493	Martin Behaim of Germany makes the oldest surviving globe; Christopher Columbus leads the first known voyage from Europe to the Americas and back again
1519–1522	Survivors of Ferdinand Magellan's expedition become the first people to sail completely around the world
1500–1800	Scientific surveying and mapmaking begin creating a clearer picture of the size and shape of Earth, the continents, and the oceans
1956	The Flat Earth Society is founded in the United States
1960s	US Navy launches the first satellites used for global positioning, the beginning of the NAVSTAR global positioning satellite network used by GPS devices

Find Out More

Books

Carey, Stephen S. *A Beginner's Guide to Scientific Method*. Independence, KY: Wadsworth, 2011.

Glass, Susan. **Prove It!** *The Scientific Method in Action*. Oxford, UK: Raintree, 2006.

Gow, Mary. *Measuring the Earth: Eratosthenes and His Celestial Geometry*. Berkeley Heights, NJ: Enslow, 2009.

Henzel, Cynthia Kennedy. *Measuring the World*. Minneapolis, MN: Checkerboard Library, 2008.

Riffenburgh, Beau. *The Men Who Mapped the World: The Treasures of Cartography*. London: Carlton Books, 2001.

Websites

How Science Works
http://kids.niehs.nih.gov/explore/scienceworks/index.htm
Part of the National Institutes of Health website, How Science Works is designed for kids and includes a summary of the scientific method.

Distinguishing Science and Pseudoscience

http://www.quackwatch.com/01QuackeryRelatedTopics/pseudo.
html

The Quackwatch site, which points out examples of bad science, includes a look at the features of good and bad science.

Who Discovered the Earth Is Round?

http://scienceblogs.com/startswithabang/2011/09/21/who
-discovered-the-earth-is-ro

ScienceBlogs, in partnership with National Geographic, presents this look at how people discovered the true shape of the world, with a detailed, illustrated account of Eratosthenes's experiment.

What Is Geodesy?

http://oceanservice.noaa.gov/education/tutorial_geodesy/
geo01_intro.html

The National Oceanic and Atmospheric Administration offers this excellent introduction to the science of measuring Earth, with pages devoted to the history of geodesy, ways of charting Earth's surface, global positioning systems (GPS), and more.

The Round Earth and Christopher Columbus

http://www.phy6.org/stargaze/Scolumb.htm

This lesson plan disproves the old myth that Columbus's sailors thought Earth was flat.

Bibliography

Ariel, Avraham and Nora Ariel Berger. *Plotting the Globe*. Westport, CT: Praeger, 2005.

Flat Earth Society homepage. http://www.alaska.net/~clund/e_djublonskopf/Flatearthsociety.htm.

Garwood, Christine. *Flat Earth: The History of an Infamous Idea*. New York: Thomas Dunne Books, 2008.

Hoare, Michael Rand. *The Quest for the True Figure of the Earth: Ideas and Expeditions in Four Centuries of Geodesy*. Burlington, VT: Ashgate Publishing, 2005.

Nicastro, Nicholas. *Circumference: Eratosthenes and the Ancient Quest to Measure the Globe*. New York: St. Martin's Press, 2008.

Russell, Jeffrey Burton. *Inventing the Flat Earth: Columbus and Modern Historians*. Westport, CT: Praeger, 1991.

Smith, James R. *Introduction to Geodesy: The History and Concepts of Modern Geodesy*. New York: Wiley Interscience, 1997.

Index

About the Author

Rebecca Stefoff has written many books for young readers on a variety of subjects: science, exploration, history, literature, and biography. She first tackled the topic of measuring and mapping Earth in *The Guide to Maps and Mapmaking* (Oxford University Press, 1995; British Library, 1995). Her books about science also include the four-volume series Humans: An Evolutionary History (Marshall Cavendish Benchmark, 2010), numerous books about animals and biology, and a biography of Charles Darwin. Stefoff lives in Portland, Oregon. You can learn more about her and her books at her website, www.rebeccastefoff.com.